The Art of Money-Making

HOW TO TURN YOUR SKILLS INTO CASH

DAMI JOSH

Copyright © 2024 by Dami Josh

TABLE OF CONTENT

INTRODUCTION

Welcome to "The Art of Money-Making: How to Turn Your Skills into Cash," a comprehensive guide designed to unlock the potential within you and transform your unique abilities into a lucrative venture. In a world where economic landscapes are constantly evolving, the ability to harness your skills for financial gain has never been more crucial. This book serves as your roadmap, offering insights, strategies, and practical tips to navigate the intricate art of monetizing your talents.

As the global economy continues to embrace digitalization and new opportunities emerge, understanding the principles of effective money-making becomes paramount. Whether you are a seasoned professional seeking to diversify your income streams or someone exploring entrepreneurial avenues for the first time, this book caters to a wide audience with actionable advice.

The Art of Money-Making is not just another get-rich-quick scheme; it's a thoughtful exploration of the symbiotic relationship between passion, skills, and financial success. Throughout these pages, you will discover how to identify your unique strengths, leverage technology, and create a sustainable income model that aligns with your personal and professional aspirations.

Drawing from real-life examples, case studies, and expert insights, this book is designed to empower you with the knowledge needed to navigate the dynamic world of entrepreneurship and monetization. Whether you are an artist, a coder, a writer, or possess any skill, this guide will help you craft a personalized roadmap to financial success.

Get ready to embark on a transformative journey as we delve into the strategies and mindset shifts required to turn your skills into a thriving source of income. "The Art of Money-Making" is not just a book; it's a tool that empowers you to take control of your financial destiny. Are you ready to unlock the doors to abundance and make your skills work for you? Let the journey begin!

CHAPTER 1: DISCOVERING YOUR UNIQUE SKILLS

Welcome to the transformative journey of self-discovery in Chapter 1: "Discovering Your Unique Skills." In the vast landscape of possibilities, each of us possesses a set of distinctive talents waiting to be unearthed and harnessed for financial gain. This chapter is a compass guiding you through the process of self-reflection, helping you identify and appreciate the unique skills that can become the cornerstone of your money-making venture.

Embarking on the path to financial success begins with a deep dive into self-awareness. As we delve into this chapter, we will explore techniques for uncovering your latent talents, conducting a thorough assessment of your strengths and weaknesses, and pinpointing the skills that set you apart. The goal is not just to recognize what you can do but to understand how these abilities can be transformed into valuable assets in the marketplace.

Discovering your unique skills is not a mere exercise in introspection; it's a critical step towards building a foundation for a fulfilling and prosperous future. Whether you are an artist, a technician, a communicator, or possess a combination of skills, this chapter provides practical tools and insights to help you recognize the potential within.

By the end of this chapter, you will gain clarity on the skills that define you and understand how they can be strategically employed to create opportunities for financial growth. So, let us embark on this journey of self-discovery together, unlocking the doors to a world where your unique skills become the currency for your success. Are you ready to unveil the treasures within? Let's begin.

- Uncovering Your Talents

Unveiling your talents is a pivotal step on the journey to financial success. In this section, we will comprehensively explore the process of uncovering your talents, emphasizing the importance of self-awareness and the methods to identify the unique gifts you bring to the table.

1. **Self-Reflection and Introspection:**

   - Begin by carving out dedicated time for self-reflection. Consider your past experiences, hobbies, and activities that genuinely bring you joy.

   - Evaluate moments where you felt a sense of accomplishment and fulfilment. These instances often serve as indicators of your natural inclinations and talents.

2. **Seeking Feedback:**

   - Engage with friends, family, and colleagues to gain external perspectives on your strengths. They might provide insights into qualities you may not have consciously recognized.

- Constructive feedback can be instrumental in identifying patterns and themes that point towards your unique talents.

3. Passion and Flow States:

- Explore activities that evoke a sense of passion and enthusiasm. Your talents are often intertwined with activities that immerse you in a state of flow, where time seems to pass effortlessly.

- Recognize the areas where you lose track of time and experience a heightened sense of focus - these are clues to your innate talents.

4. Skills Assessment Tools:

- Leverage various skills assessment tools available online. These tools can provide structured assessments, offering insights into your strengths, weaknesses, and potential areas for growth.

- Assessments like StrengthsFinder, Myers-Briggs Type Indicator (MBTI), or DISC profiling can offer valuable perspectives on your unique traits.

5. Embracing Versatility:

- Acknowledge that talents can manifest in diverse forms. While some talents may be overt, others might be subtle and versatile.

- Embrace the multidimensionality of your skills, recognizing that a combination of abilities can form a unique skill set that sets you apart.

6. Learning and Exploration:

- Be open to new experiences and continuously seek opportunities to learn. New skills and interests may surface, adding layers to your talent profile.

- Embrace a growth mindset, understanding that talents can evolve and expand with ongoing learning and development.

Uncovering your talents is an ongoing, dynamic process. It requires a blend of introspection, external feedback, and a willingness to explore uncharted territories. As you progress in this journey, remember that self-discovery is a continual evolution, and your talents are the seeds of your financial prosperity. Embrace the uniqueness that defines you, and let your uncovered talents pave the way for a fulfilling and lucrative future.

- Assessing Your Strengths and Weaknesses

Understanding your strengths and weaknesses is a fundamental aspect of personal and professional development. This process of self-assessment is crucial for building a successful money-making venture. In this comprehensive guide, we will explore the methods and significance of assessing your strengths and weaknesses.

1. **Reflective Analysis:**

   - Begin by reflecting on your past experiences, both in your personal and professional life. Identify instances where you excelled and felt a sense of accomplishment.

   - Delve into challenges you've faced and discern the skills or qualities that helped you overcome them.

2. Skill Inventory:

   - Create a comprehensive inventory of your skills. Categorize them into technical, soft, and transferable skills.

   - Consider skills acquired through formal education, on-the-job experiences, or personal hobbies. This inventory provides a snapshot of your capabilities.

3. Feedback Mechanism:

   - Seek feedback from peers, mentors, and colleagues. Others often observe strengths that you may not recognize in yourself.

   - Constructive criticism is equally valuable. Embrace feedback on areas where improvement is needed to refine your self-awareness.

4. **SWOT Analysis:**

  - Conduct a SWOT (Strengths, Weaknesses, Opportunities, Threats) analysis. Identify internal factors (strengths and weaknesses) and external factors (opportunities and threats) that may impact your entrepreneurial journey.

  - This structured analysis aids in strategic planning by highlighting areas for optimization and potential avenues for growth.

5. **Embrace Diverse Perspectives:**

  - Recognize that strengths and weaknesses are often context-dependent. A skill beneficial in one scenario may not be as advantageous in another.

  - Embrace the diversity of perspectives by considering how your strengths align with the specific requirements of your chosen money-making venture.

6. **Continuous Improvement:**

  - Understand that self-assessment is an ongoing process. Regularly revisit and update your assessment as you acquire new skills and experiences.

- Cultivate a mindset of continuous improvement, acknowledging that weaknesses can be transformed into strengths through focused effort and learning.

7. Alignment with Goals:

- Evaluate your strengths and weaknesses about your financial goals. Ensure that your skill set aligns with the demands of your chosen industry or market.

- Identify areas where leveraging strengths can provide a competitive advantage and where addressing weaknesses is essential for success.

8. Holistic Approach:

- Take a holistic approach by considering not only technical skills but also emotional intelligence, adaptability, and communication skills.

- Recognize that a well-rounded set of strengths contributes to a more resilient and adaptable entrepreneurial journey.

Assessing your strengths and weaknesses is a strategic process that lays the foundation for informed decision-making and goal-setting. By gaining clarity on your capabilities, you empower yourself to leverage strengths, address weaknesses, and navigate the challenges of turning your skills into a lucrative venture. Embrace this process as a vital step toward building a successful and fulfilling money-making endeavor.

- Identifying Marketable Skills

Identifying marketable skills is a pivotal step in transforming your abilities into a sustainable source of income. This process involves a thorough exploration of your skill set and an understanding of how those skills align with current market demands. Here's a comprehensive guide to help you navigate the process:

1. **Self-Reflection:**

   - Begin by reflecting on the skills you enjoy using and those that bring you a sense of accomplishment. Consider activities where you effortlessly demonstrate proficiency.

   - Identify skills that have been valuable in previous roles or projects, recognizing the areas where you excel.

2. **Industry Research:**

   - Stay informed about industry trends and emerging markets. Research the skills in demand by analyzing job postings, industry reports, and discussions in relevant communities.

   - Identify the intersection between your existing skills and those sought after in the market to pinpoint potential opportunities.

3. **Networking and Conversations**:

   - Engage in conversations with professionals in your field of interest. Attend industry events, and webinars, or join online communities to understand the skills valued by successful individuals.

- Networking provides valuable insights into the skills that have contributed to the success of others in similar ventures.

4. Skills Assessment Tools:

- Utilize skills assessment tools or platforms that match your skills with market demand. Websites like LinkedIn Learning, Skill share, or industry-specific platforms often offer assessments to identify marketable skills.

- Assessments provide an objective analysis, highlighting areas where your skills align with current market needs.

5. Diversification and Specialization:

- Evaluate the diversity of your skill set. Consider both specialized skills that set you apart and broad skills that offer versatility.

- Find a balance between being a specialist in a niche area and possessing transferable skills that appeal to a broader audience.

6. **Feedback from Clients or Peers:**

- If applicable, gather feedback from clients, customers, or peers who have experienced your work. Understand which skills they find most valuable and how your offerings meet their needs.

- Client feedback can provide valuable insights into the marketability of your skills.

7. **Continuous Learning:**

- Stay committed to continuous learning and skill development. Markets evolve, and staying current enhances your adaptability to changing demands.

- Identify emerging skills in your industry and invest time in acquiring them to stay ahead of the curve.

8. **Personal Branding:**

- Develop a strong personal brand that aligns with your marketable skills. Communicate your unique value proposition and how your skills address the needs of your target audience.

- Crafting a compelling personal brand enhances your visibility and credibility in the market.

9. **Testing and Iteration:**

- Test the marketability of your skills through small projects, freelance work, or pilot programs. Gather feedback from clients and adjust your approach based on the response.

- Iteration is key to refining your offerings and ensuring they resonate with your target audience.

Identifying marketable skills is a dynamic process that requires a blend of self-awareness, market research, and adaptability. By aligning your skills with market demands, you position yourself for success in turning your talents into a thriving business. Embrace this journey of discovery and refinement as you build a compelling portfolio of marketable skills.

CHAPTER 2: THE ENTREPRENEURIAL MINDSET

Welcome to the exploration of a fundamental aspect of your journey to financial success—Chapter 2: "The Entrepreneurial Mindset." In the dynamic landscape of turning your skills into a thriving source of income, cultivating the right mindset is akin to laying a sturdy foundation for a successful venture. This chapter delves into the essential qualities and perspectives that define an entrepreneurial mindset, guiding you on a transformative path toward realizing your financial aspirations.

Entrepreneurship extends beyond mere business acumen; it's a mindset that embraces innovation, resilience, and a willingness to navigate the uncertainties that come with pursuing your passion. As we embark on this chapter, we'll unravel the intricacies of what it truly means to adopt an entrepreneurial mindset—how it shapes your decision-making, propels you to embrace challenges, and empowers you to turn setbacks into opportunities.

The entrepreneurial mindset is a mindset of growth, adaptability, and a relentless pursuit of goals. It involves cultivating a positive outlook toward risk, embracing failure as a stepping stone to success, and fostering creativity that propels you to think beyond conventional boundaries. Through practical insights, real-world examples, and actionable strategies, this chapter will equip you with the tools needed to nurture and embody the entrepreneurial spirit.

Whether you are a seasoned entrepreneur seeking to fine-tune your mindset or someone stepping into the entrepreneurial realm for the first time, the principles discussed in this chapter are universal. By the end of this exploration, you'll not only understand the core tenets of the entrepreneurial mindset but also be prepared to integrate them into your daily life and business endeavours. Are you ready to embrace the mindset that transforms challenges into opportunities and dreams into reality? Let the journey into the entrepreneurial mindset commence.

- Cultivating a Positive Money-Making Mindset

A positive money-making mindset is the cornerstone of entrepreneurial success, influencing decision-making, resilience, and the ability to transform challenges into opportunities. This comprehensive guide delves into the key components of cultivating a positive mindset for financial success.

1. **Mindfulness and Awareness:**

   - Cultivate mindfulness to stay present and aware of your thoughts and emotions. Mindfulness allows you to observe negative thought patterns and replace them with positive affirmations.

- Awareness of your mindset is the first step towards cultivating a positive approach to money-making endeavors.

2. **Optimism and Positivity:**

- Foster an optimistic outlook by focusing on opportunities rather than obstacles. Embrace challenges as stepping stones to growth and learning.

- Develop a habit of framing situations positively, emphasizing what can be gained from every experience.

3. **Gratitude and Abundance Mentality:**

- Practice gratitude for the skills, opportunities, and resources at your disposal. A grateful mindset fosters a sense of abundance, shifting your focus from scarcity to prosperity.

- Embrace an abundance mentality, believing that there are ample opportunities for success and that your achievements do not diminish others.

4. **Risk-Taking and Fear Resilience:**

- Embrace calculated risks as essential components of entrepreneurial endeavors. A positive money-making mindset views risk as an avenue for growth rather than a threat.

- Develop resilience in the face of fear. Recognize that fear is a natural part of the entrepreneurial journey and use it as fuel for innovation and progress.

5. **Goal Setting and Visualization:**

- Set clear, achievable goals and visualize your success. Visualization creates a positive mental image of your financial aspirations, reinforcing your commitment and motivation.

- Break down larger goals into smaller, manageable tasks, celebrating each accomplishment along the way.

6. **Continuous Learning and Adaptability:**

   - Cultivate a growth mindset by embracing continuous learning. View challenges as opportunities to acquire new skills and knowledge.

   - Stay adaptable in the face of change. A positive mindset sees change as a chance for innovation and improvement, rather than a disruption.

7. **Self-Confidence and Self-Efficacy:**

   - Build self-confidence by acknowledging your achievements and capabilities. A positive money-making mindset thrives on self-belief.

   - Develop self-efficacy—the belief in your ability to execute specific tasks. Break down complex challenges into manageable steps, reinforcing a sense of competence.

8. **Network and Collaboration:**

   - Surround yourself with a positive, supportive network. Engage with individuals who share a similar mindset and are enthusiastic about your financial journey.

- Collaborate with like-minded individuals to leverage collective strengths and insights. Positive collaboration enhances creativity and problem-solving.

9. **Celebrate Progress, Learn from Setbacks:**

- Celebrate your achievements, no matter how small. Positive reinforcement strengthens your commitment to your money-making goals.

- View setbacks as opportunities to learn and grow. A positive mindset perceives setbacks as temporary obstacles, not insurmountable failures.

Cultivating a positive money-making mindset is an ongoing process that involves intentional effort and a commitment to personal growth. By integrating these principles into your daily life, you'll create a mental foundation that propels you towards financial success, fostering resilience, creativity, and an unwavering belief in your ability to turn your skills into a lucrative venture.

- Embracing Risk and Overcoming Fear

Embracing risk and overcoming fear are integral components of the entrepreneurial mindset, crucial for transforming skills into a lucrative venture. This comprehensive guide delves into the key facets of understanding and navigating risk, as well as strategies for overcoming fear on the path to financial success.

1. Understanding Risk:

- **Calculated Risk vs. Blind Risk:** Differentiate between calculated risks, where potential benefits are weighed against potential drawbacks, and blind risks, which are impulsive and lack strategic assessment.

- **Risk Tolerance:** Assess your risk tolerance by evaluating your comfort level with uncertainty. Recognize that a healthy level of risk is often necessary for innovation and growth.

2. **Shifting Perspective on Failure:**

   - **Learning Opportunities:** Reframe failure as a learning opportunity rather than a definitive setback. Embrace failures as stepping stones towards refinement and improvement.

   - **Iterative Process:** Understand that entrepreneurship is often an iterative process, where failures contribute to the evolution of ideas and strategies.

3. **Strategic Decision-Making:**

   - **Risk Mitigation:** Implement strategies to mitigate potential risks. This involves thorough research, scenario planning, and developing contingency plans.

   - **Informed Decision-Making:** Make decisions based on informed analysis rather than impulsive reactions. A strategic approach minimizes unforeseen risks.

4. Fear Identification and Acknowledgment:

- **Recognizing Fear:** Identify specific fears related to your entrepreneurial journey. Isolate and name the fears to bring them into conscious awareness.

- **Normalizing Fear:** Understand that fear is a natural part of the entrepreneurial process. Normalizing fear reduces its paralyzing effects.

5. Mindfulness and Fear Resilience:

- **Mindfulness Practices:** Engage in mindfulness practices such as meditation and deep breathing to manage fear-induced stress. Mindfulness enhances resilience and emotional regulation.

- **Positive Affirmations:** Use positive affirmations to counteract negative thoughts and instill confidence. Affirmations contribute to a positive mindset that can withstand fear.

6. Incremental Exposure:

- **Gradual Exposure:** Gradually expose yourself to situations that trigger fear. Incremental exposure helps desensitize fear responses and builds resilience over time.

- **Celebrating Small Wins:** Acknowledge and celebrate small successes achieved through overcoming fears. Celebrating victories reinforces a positive mindset.

7. Community Support:

- **Peer Networks:** Engage with supportive entrepreneurial communities. Sharing fears and challenges with peers fosters a sense of camaraderie and provides valuable insights.

- **Mentorship:** Seek mentorship from individuals who have navigated similar challenges. Mentors can offer guidance and perspective, easing fear through shared experiences.

8. Visualization and Positive Imagery:

- **Visualization Techniques:** Visualize successful outcomes and positive scenarios related to your entrepreneurial pursuits. Visualization prepares the mind for success and reduces fear.

- **Positive Imagery:** Surround yourself with positive imagery that reflects your goals. Images of success create a mental environment conducive to overcoming fear.

9. Continuous Learning:

- **Knowledge Empowerment:** Deepen your understanding of your industry and market. Knowledge empowers you to make informed decisions, reducing fear associated with uncertainty.

- **Skill Development:** Acquire new skills to bolster your confidence. The continuous development of skills fosters a sense of competence that combats fear.

Embracing risk and overcoming fear require a strategic blend of mindset shifts, practical strategies, and a commitment to personal growth. By integrating these principles into your entrepreneurial journey, you'll not only navigate risks with greater confidence but also transform fear into a catalyst for innovation and success. This dynamic approach positions you to embrace uncertainty, adapt to challenges, and ultimately turn your skills into a flourishing source of income.

- Learning from Failure and Adaptation

Failure is an inevitable aspect of the entrepreneurial journey, but its transformative power lies in the ability to learn and adapt. This comprehensive guide explores the process of learning from failure, emphasizing adaptation as a key driver for entrepreneurial success.

1. **Cultivating a Growth Mindset:**

   - **Embrace Challenges as Opportunities:** Adopt a growth mindset that views challenges and failures as opportunities for learning and improvement. See setbacks as a natural part of the entrepreneurial process.

   - **Belief in Development:** Cultivate a belief that abilities can be developed through dedication and hard work. This mindset fosters resilience and a positive approach to failure.

2. Post-Failure Reflection:

- **Analyzing Root Causes:** After a failure, conduct a thorough analysis to understand the root causes. Identify specific factors that contributed to the setback.

- **Avoiding Attribution Errors:** Avoid attributing failure solely to external factors. Recognize the role of internal factors and decisions in the outcome.

3. Extracting Lessons and Insights:

- **Identify Takeaways:** Extract valuable lessons from each failure. Consider what worked well, what didn't, and why.

- **Feedback Gathering:** Seek feedback from peers, mentors, or customers. External perspectives provide insights that might be overlooked internally.

4. Iterative Problem-Solving:

- **Iterate Solutions:** Develop an iterative problem-solving approach. Implement changes based on the lessons learned, creating an environment where failure leads to continuous improvement.

- **Pilot Programs:** Test new strategies through small-scale pilot programs before full-scale implementation. This allows for controlled experimentation and adjustment.

5. Flexibility and Adaptability:

- **Openness to Change:** Embrace a mindset that is open to change. Recognize that adaptability is a strength and that rigid adherence to initial plans may hinder progress.

- **Quick Decision-Making:** Develop the ability to make decisions promptly in response to new information. Agility and adaptability are critical in dynamic entrepreneurial environments.

6. **Emotional Resilience:**

- **Separating Self-Worth from Failure:** Cultivate emotional resilience by separating personal identity from business outcomes. Understand that failure in a venture doesn't equate to personal failure.

- **Mindfulness Practices:** Engage in mindfulness practices to manage stress and anxiety associated with failure. Mindfulness enhances emotional regulation and clarity of thought.

7. **Seeking Mentorship:**

- **Guidance from Experienced Mentors:** Seek mentorship from individuals who have navigated failure and achieved success. Mentors provide valuable guidance, share their experiences, and offer perspective.

- **Peer Learning:** Engage with peer networks where entrepreneurs share their failure stories. Peer learning creates a supportive environment and reduces the stigma associated with failure.

8. **Building Resilient Teams:**

   - **Encouraging a Culture of Learning:** Foster a culture within your team that encourages learning from failure. Create an environment where team members feel comfortable sharing setbacks and ideas for improvement.

   - **Team Feedback Sessions:** Conduct regular team feedback sessions to collectively analyze failures and brainstorm adaptive strategies. Shared insights enhance team resilience.

9. **Celebrating Adaptation Success:**

   - **Acknowledging Adaptive Wins:** Celebrate successes resulting from adaptive strategies. Recognize and commend the team's ability to learn from failure, adapt, and pivot towards success.

   - **Positive Reinforcement:** Reinforce the idea that learning from failure and adapting is integral to long-term success. Positive reinforcement encourages a proactive approach to overcoming setbacks.

10. Continuous Learning Loop:

   - Embedding a Learning Culture: Infuse a learning culture into the fabric of your entrepreneurial venture. Emphasize the importance of continuous learning, adaptation, and improvement.

   - Feedback Integration: Continuously integrate feedback loops into your processes. Regularly revisit and refine strategies based on ongoing learning experiences.

Learning from failure and adaptation is not a linear process but rather a continuous loop of improvement. By embracing failure as a catalyst for growth, entrepreneurs can transform setbacks into stepping stones toward success. Through a combination of mindset shifts, reflective practices, and adaptive strategies, the entrepreneurial journey becomes a dynamic evolution, positioning individuals and teams to navigate challenges successfully and turn their skills into a resilient and flourishing venture.

CHAPTER 3: LEVERAGING TECHNOLOGY FOR SUCCESS

Welcome to the dynamic exploration of Chapter 3: "Leveraging Technology for Success." In the contemporary landscape of money-making ventures, technology stands as a powerful catalyst, offering unprecedented opportunities for innovation, efficiency, and global reach. This chapter is your guide to understanding how harnessing the capabilities of technology can elevate your entrepreneurial journey and propel your skills into the realms of success.

As we step into this chapter, we'll embark on a journey through the digital landscape, exploring the myriad ways technology can be strategically employed to augment your business endeavors.

From establishing a robust online presence to tapping into the vast potential of e-commerce, this chapter unfolds a comprehensive playbook for integrating technology seamlessly into your money-making strategy.

Technology is not just a tool; it's a transformative force that can amplify your impact, enhance your reach, and revolutionize the way you turn your skills into a lucrative venture. Whether you are a tech-savvy entrepreneur or someone navigating the digital realm for the first time, the insights within this chapter are designed to demystify technology and empower you to wield its potential with confidence.

Get ready to unravel the possibilities that technology presents for your financial success. From leveraging data analytics to embracing automation and understanding the nuances of online marketing, this chapter will equip you with the knowledge and strategies needed to thrive in the digital age.

Are you prepared to embrace the technological frontier and unlock the doors to unprecedented opportunities? Let's dive into the transformative realm of "Leveraging Technology for Success" and discover how it can shape the trajectory of your entrepreneurial journey. The future is digital, and the possibilities are limitless—let's explore them together.

- Harnessing the Power of the Digital Age

In the contemporary landscape of entrepreneurship, mastering the art of harnessing the power of the digital age is essential for turning skills into a successful and scalable venture. This comprehensive guide delves into the multifaceted process of leveraging technology to propel your money-making endeavors to new heights.

1. **Building a Robust Online Presence:**

   - **Website Development:** Create a professional and user-friendly website to serve as the digital hub for your venture. Optimize it for search engines and user experience.

  - **Social Media Platforms:** Establish a strong presence on relevant social media platforms. Leverage these channels to engage with your audience, share content, and build a community around your brand.

2. **E-commerce Strategies:**

  - **Online Marketplaces:** Explore popular online marketplaces such as Amazon, Etsy, or eBay, depending on your niche. Leverage these platforms to reach a broader audience.

  - **E-commerce Website:** Consider setting up your e-commerce website for direct sales. Ensure seamless navigation, secure transactions, and personalized user experiences.

3. **Digital Marketing and SEO:**

  - **Content Marketing:** Develop a content marketing strategy to create valuable, shareable content. Blog posts, videos, and infographics can enhance your online presence and attract a targeted audience.

   - **Search Engine Optimization (SEO):** Optimize your digital content for search engines to improve visibility. Keyword research, meta tags, and quality content contribute to higher search engine rankings.

4. Data Analytics for Informed Decision-Making:

   - **Implementing Analytics Tools:** Integrate analytics tools such as Google Analytics to track user behavior, website traffic, and conversion rates. Analyzing data provides insights for informed decision-making.

   - **A/B Testing:** Conduct A/B testing to optimize digital campaigns. Test variations of content, design, or user interface elements to identify the most effective strategies.

5. Automation for Efficiency:

   - **Email Marketing Automation:** Implement email marketing automation to nurture leads and engage with your audience. Automation streamlines communication and ensures timely responses.

- **Workflow Automation:** Explore tools for workflow automation to enhance operational efficiency. Automation can simplify repetitive tasks, allowing you to focus on strategic aspects of your business.

6. Cybersecurity Measures:

- **Secure Transactions:** Prioritize cybersecurity to ensure secure online transactions and protect sensitive customer information. Utilize secure payment gateways and SSL certificates for data encryption.

- **Employee Training:** Educate your team about cybersecurity best practices to prevent data breaches. Vigilance and knowledge are crucial in safeguarding your digital assets.

7. Mobile Optimization:

- **Responsive Design:** Optimize your digital assets for mobile devices. Responsive design ensures a seamless and enjoyable user experience across various screen sizes.

- **Mobile Apps:** Consider developing a mobile app if it aligns with your business model. Apps can enhance user engagement and provide a convenient platform for transactions.

8. Integration of Emerging Technologies:

- **Blockchain Technology:** Explore the integration of blockchain for enhanced security and transparency, especially in industries like finance or supply chain.

- **Artificial Intelligence (AI) and Machine Learning (ML):** Consider applications of AI and ML for data analysis, customer personalization, and process automation to gain a competitive edge.

9. Continuous Adaptation to Technological Trends:

- **Staying Informed:** Stay abreast of emerging technological trends. Regularly assess how new technologies can enhance your business model and contribute to your overall strategy.

- **Agile Approach:** Adopt an agile approach to technology adoption. Be ready to pivot and adapt to technological advancements that align with your business goals.

10. **Compliance with Digital Regulations:**

- **Data Privacy Compliance:** Adhere to data privacy regulations such as GDPR or CCPA. Prioritize customer data protection and communicate transparently about your privacy practices.

- **Digital Security Standards:** Implement industry-specific digital security standards to protect your business and customer information.

Harnessing the power of the digital age is a dynamic and ongoing process. By strategically integrating these practices into your entrepreneurial journey, you position yourself to thrive in the ever-evolving digital landscape. Embrace the opportunities that technology presents, innovate with purpose, and let the digital age become a transformative force in turning your skills into a flourishing and sustainable venture.

- Building an Online Presence

In the digital age, establishing a robust online presence is a cornerstone of entrepreneurial success. This comprehensive guide explores the multifaceted process of building an online presence, encompassing website development, social media strategies, and content marketing to enhance visibility, engagement, and credibility.

1. **Website Development:**

   - **Strategic Planning:** Define the purpose and goals of your website. Whether it's an e-commerce platform, a portfolio, or an informational site, clarity on objectives guides the design and content.

   - **User-Centric Design:** Prioritize user experience (UX) and design a website that is intuitive, aesthetically pleasing, and responsive across devices.

- **Optimized Content:** Craft compelling and SEO-optimized content for each page. Incorporate relevant keywords to enhance search engine visibility.

2. **Social Media Platforms:**

- **Target Audience Analysis:** Identify the social media platforms most frequented by your target audience. Tailor your presence based on the demographics and preferences of your potential customers.

- **Consistent Branding:** Maintain a consistent brand image across all platforms. Utilize professional imagery, cohesive messaging, and a recognizable logo.

- **Engagement Strategies:** Foster audience engagement through regular posting, responding to comments, and participating in discussions. Utilize polls, contests, and other interactive content.

3. Content Marketing Strategy:

- **Identifying Content Types:** Diversify content types, including blog posts, videos, infographics, and podcasts. Adapt your content to suit the preferences of your audience.

- **Consistent Publishing:** Establish a content calendar for consistent publishing. Regular, high-quality content enhances your credibility and keeps your audience engaged.

- **Guest Blogging and Collaborations:** Explore opportunities for guest blogging on relevant platforms or collaborations with influencers. This expands your reach and introduces your brand to new audiences.

4. Email Marketing Campaigns:

- **Building Subscribers:** Create incentives for visitors to subscribe to your email list. Offer exclusive content, discounts, or newsletters to build a loyal subscriber base.

- **Segmentation and Personalization:** Segment your email list based on customer preferences and demographics. Personalize content to cater to specific audience segments.

- **Automation for Efficiency:** Implement email automation to streamline campaigns. Automation can include welcome sequences, follow-ups, and personalized recommendations.

5. Search Engine Optimization (SEO):

- **Keyword Research:** Conduct thorough keyword research to identify phrases relevant to your business. Incorporate these keywords naturally into your website content for better search engine rankings.

- **Backlink Building:** Develop a backlink strategy by obtaining high-quality, relevant backlinks. Backlinks enhance your website's authority and improve search engine visibility.

- **Technical SEO:** Optimize technical aspects such as website speed, mobile-friendliness, and site structure. Technical SEO contributes to a positive user experience and better search rankings.

6. Online Reputation Management:

- **Monitoring Brand Mentions:** Regularly monitor mentions of your brand across online platforms. Respond promptly to customer reviews, both positive and negative.

- **Authenticity and Transparency:** Build trust by being authentic and transparent in your online interactions. Address customer concerns openly and showcase your commitment to customer satisfaction.

7. Visual Content and Multimedia:

- **High-Quality Imagery:** Utilize high-quality images and graphics on your website and social media. Visual appeal enhances the user experience and communicates professionalism.

- **Video Content:** Incorporate video content to convey messages effectively. Video marketing is a powerful tool for engagement and storytelling.

8. Analytics and Measurement:

 - **Setting Metrics:** Define key performance indicators (KPIs) aligned with your online presence goals. These may include website traffic, social media engagement, conversion rates, and more.

 - **Regular Performance Analysis:** Utilize analytics tools to regularly assess the performance of your online presence. Adjust strategies based on data insights to optimize results.

9. Mobile Optimization:

 - **Responsive Design:** Ensure your website is optimized for mobile devices. Responsive design guarantees a seamless and enjoyable user experience across smartphones and tablets.

 - **Mobile-Friendly Content:** Tailor your content for mobile consumption. Consider the shorter attention spans of mobile users and present information concisely.

10. **Adaptation to Emerging Trends:**

- **Stay Informed:** Keep abreast of emerging trends and technologies in online presence strategies. Attend webinars, read industry publications, and participate in relevant forums.

- **Adopt New Platforms:** Embrace new social media platforms or emerging technologies that align with your brand and audience. Early adoption can provide a competitive edge.

Building an online presence is not a one-time effort but an ongoing process of adaptation and refinement. By implementing these strategies and staying attuned to the evolving digital landscape, you can create a compelling online presence that enhances brand visibility, fosters customer engagement, and ultimately contributes to the success of your money-making venture.

- E-Commerce Opportunities

In the ever-expanding digital landscape, e-commerce presents a myriad of opportunities for entrepreneurs to transform skills into lucrative ventures. This comprehensive guide explores the diverse avenues and strategies within the realm of e-commerce, ranging from online marketplaces to creating your e-commerce website.

1. **Online Marketplaces:**

   - **Amazon, eBay, Etsy:** Explore well-established online marketplaces like Amazon, eBay, and Etsy. These platforms provide access to a vast customer base and offer a streamlined infrastructure for product listings, transactions, and shipping.

   - **Niche Marketplaces:** Consider specialized marketplaces that cater to specific niches. Platforms like Houzz for home goods or Zibbet for handmade items can provide targeted exposure.

2. Establishing Your E-Commerce Website:

- **Selecting a Platform:** Choose a suitable e-commerce platform based on your business needs. Options like Shopify, WooCommerce (for WordPress users), and Magento offer varied features and scalability.

- **Design and User Experience:** Prioritize an intuitive design and user experience. Optimize for mobile responsiveness to accommodate the increasing number of mobile shoppers.

- **Secure Payment Gateways:** Integrate secure payment gateways to ensure smooth and safe transactions. Options like PayPal, Stripe, and Square offer reliable solutions.

3. Dropshipping:

- **Low-Capital Model:** Consider dropshipping as a low-capital e-commerce model. With this approach, you partner with suppliers who handle inventory and fulfilment, allowing you to focus on marketing and sales.

- **Risk Mitigation:** Dropshipping minimizes the risk of unsold inventory, as you only purchase items when a customer makes a purchase.

4. Print-on-Demand Services:

- **Custom Merchandise:** Utilize print-on-demand services to create custom merchandise. Products like T-shirts, mugs, and phone cases can be produced and shipped on-demand, reducing upfront costs.

- **Design Partnerships:** Collaborate with designers or use design tools to create unique and marketable products. Print-on-demand services handle production and shipping.

5. Subscription Box Services:

- **Curated Products:** Launch a subscription box service offering curated products. This model provides recurring revenue and fosters customer loyalty.

- **Personalization:** Tailor subscription boxes to customer preferences, enhancing the personalized experience and encouraging long-term subscriptions.

6. Digital Products and Services:

- **E-Books, Courses, and Consultations:** Leverage e-commerce for digital products and services. Sell e-books, online courses, or consulting services directly through your website.

- **Global Reach:** Digital products provide a scalable business model with the potential for a global customer base.

7. B2B E-Commerce:

- **Wholesale Platforms:** Explore B2B e-commerce opportunities by offering products at wholesale prices. Platforms like Alibaba or specialized B2B marketplaces connect businesses in bulk transactions.

- **Streamlined Procurement:** Provide a streamlined procurement process for businesses, offering bulk purchasing, customized quotes, and efficient order management.

8. **Social Commerce:**

- **Social Media Selling:** Leverage social media platforms for direct selling. Platforms like Facebook Shops and Instagram Shopping enable businesses to showcase products and facilitate transactions directly within the social environment.

- **Influencer Collaborations:** Partner with influencers for social commerce. Influencers can showcase and promote your products to their engaged audiences.

9. **Global Expansion and Cross-Border E-Commerce:**

- **Market Research:** Explore opportunities for global expansion. Conduct market research to identify demand in international markets.

- **Logistics and Regulations:** Address logistics and regulatory considerations for cross-border e-commerce. Streamline shipping processes and adhere to international trade regulations.

10. **AI and Personalization:**

  - **AI-Powered Recommendations:** Implement AI algorithms for personalized product recommendations. This enhances the customer shopping experience and increases the likelihood of cross-selling.

  - **Chatbots for Customer Service:** Integrate chatbots for customer service. AI-driven chatbots provide instant support and can handle routine inquiries, improving efficiency.

11. **Sustainable E-Commerce Practices:**

  - **Eco-Friendly Packaging:** Embrace sustainability in e-commerce practices. Utilize eco-friendly packaging, reduce waste, and communicate your commitment to environmental responsibility.

  - **Transparency:** Communicate transparently about the sustainability practices of your products. Eco-conscious consumers are increasingly seeking products aligned with their values.

12. Augmented Reality (AR) for Product Visualization:

- **Virtual Try-Ons:** Implement AR for virtual try-ons or product visualizations. This technology enhances the online shopping experience, particularly for products like apparel, accessories, and furniture.

- **Reducing Returns:** AR-powered product visualization reduces the likelihood of returns by providing customers with a more accurate representation of the products.

E-commerce opportunities are dynamic and diverse, offering entrepreneurs various avenues to turn their skills into successful ventures. By understanding the nuances of different e-commerce models and staying attuned to industry trends, entrepreneurs can strategically navigate this digital landscape, ensuring not only financial success but also a scalable and sustainable business in the ever-evolving e-commerce ecosystem.

CHAPTER 4: CRAFTING YOUR MONEY-MAKING STRATEGY

Welcome to the transformative journey of Chapter 4: "Crafting Your Money-Making Strategy." In the intricate tapestry of entrepreneurial success, your strategy serves as the guiding thread, weaving together your skills, insights, and innovative approaches into a roadmap for financial prosperity. This chapter is a deep dive into the art and science of crafting a strategic plan tailored to turn your unique abilities into a thriving venture.

As we embark on this chapter, we'll unravel the essential components of a money-making strategy that transcends the ordinary. From understanding market dynamics to identifying your competitive advantage, we'll explore the strategic framework that aligns your skills with lucrative opportunities. Whether you're a seasoned entrepreneur refining your strategy or someone setting out on the entrepreneurial path for the first time, the principles within this chapter are designed to empower you with the knowledge and tools needed to create a robust and adaptive money-making strategy.

Crafting your money-making strategy is not a one-size-fits-all endeavor; it's a personalized and dynamic process that requires careful consideration of your skills, market trends, and your unique value proposition. Through practical insights, case studies, and actionable steps, this chapter will guide you in crafting a strategy that not only navigates challenges but also capitalizes on the ever-changing landscape of the business world.

Are you ready to delve into the strategic realm of turning your skills into a lucrative venture? Let the exploration of "Crafting Your Money-Making Strategy" commence, as we unveil the secrets to building a strategic foundation that propels you towards sustainable success in the dynamic landscape of entrepreneurship.

- Developing a Personalized Income Model

Creating a personalized income model is a crucial step in crafting a sustainable and lucrative money-making strategy. This comprehensive guide delves into the key considerations and strategies involved in developing a personalized income model tailored to your skills, goals, and the ever-evolving market landscape.

1. **Self-Assessment and Skill Inventory:**

   - **Identify Core Competencies:** Begin by conducting a thorough self-assessment to identify your core competencies and skills. What are you exceptionally good at? What unique talents do you possess?

- **Passion Alignment:** Align your income model with your passions. Identifying areas where your skills intersect with your interests fosters sustained motivation and enthusiasm.

2. Market Research and Trend Analysis:

- **Identify Market Needs:** Conduct market research to understand current needs and trends. Identify gaps or opportunities where your skills can provide valuable solutions.

- **Competitive Landscape:** Analyze the competitive landscape to position your income model uniquely. Identify competitors, study their approaches, and find areas for differentiation.

3. Diversification Strategies:

- **Multiple Income Streams:** Explore diversification by developing multiple income streams. This could include combining product sales, services, consulting, or other revenue-generating activities.

- **Risk Mitigation:** Diversification not only enhances income potential but also mitigates risks associated with dependency on a single source.

4. Value Proposition and Unique Selling Proposition (USP):

- **Define Your Value:** Clearly articulate the value you provide to your target audience. What sets you apart from others in your field? Develop a compelling Unique Selling Proposition (USP).

- **Customer-Centric Approach:** Ensure your income model addresses specific pain points or desires of your target customers. A customer-centric approach enhances the perceived value of your offerings.

5. Monetizing Skills and Expertise:

- **Consulting and Coaching:** Offer consulting or coaching services based on your expertise. Many individuals and businesses are willing to pay for personalized guidance and insights.

- **Online Courses and Workshops:** Monetize your knowledge by creating and selling online courses or workshops. Platforms like Udemy and Teachable provide avenues for course delivery.

6. Product Development and Sales:

- **Physical Products:** If applicable, consider developing and selling physical products. E-commerce platforms or partnerships with existing retailers can facilitate product sales.

- **Digital Products:** Explore the creation of digital products such as e-books, software, or digital art. Digital products offer scalability and minimal distribution costs.

7. Freelancing and Contract Work:

- **Freelance Platforms:** Explore freelancing opportunities on platforms like Upwork, Fiverr, or Freelancer. Offer your skills and services on a project basis to a diverse client base.

- Contractual Agreements: Seek longer-term contracts or retainer agreements with clients. This provides a more stable income stream compared to one-off projects.

8. Subscription and Membership Models:

- **Subscription Services:** Consider offering subscription-based services or products. This could include a monthly newsletter, exclusive content, or ongoing access to your expertise.

- **Membership Communities:** Create membership communities where individuals pay for exclusive access to a network, resources, or expertise. This model fosters community engagement and recurring revenue.

9. Affiliate Marketing and Partnerships:

- **Affiliate Programs:** Explore affiliate marketing opportunities where you promote products or services and earn a commission for each sale generated through your referral.

- **Strategic Partnerships:** Form strategic partnerships with other businesses or individuals.

Collaborate on joint ventures or co-create products to expand your reach and income potential.

10. **Automation and Passive Income:**

   - **Automated Systems:** Integrate automation into your income model where possible. This may involve automated sales funnels, email campaigns, or other systems that require minimal ongoing manual effort.

   - **Passive Income Streams:** Aim to develop passive income streams that generate revenue with minimal day-to-day involvement. This could be through investments, royalties, or automated digital products.

11. **Financial Planning and Goal Setting:**

   - **Clear Financial Goals:** Define clear financial goals for your income model. Set short-term and long-term objectives, considering both revenue targets and personal financial aspirations.

   - **Budgeting and Savings:** Implement effective budgeting and savings strategies. Ensure that your income model aligns with your lifestyle and financial requirements.

12. **Adaptation and Continuous Improvement:**

- **Market Monitoring:** Regularly monitor market trends, customer feedback, and changes in your industry. Stay adaptable and be prepared to adjust your income model based on evolving conditions.

- **Feedback Integration:** Solicit feedback from customers and clients. Use constructive feedback to refine your offerings and improve the value you provide.

Developing a personalized income model is an iterative process that requires a combination of self-awareness, market understanding, and strategic creativity. By aligning your skills with market demands, diversifying income streams, and staying attuned to emerging opportunities, you can craft a dynamic income model that not only sustains your financial goals but also evolves with the changing landscape of your industry.

- Setting Realistic Financial Goals

Establishing realistic financial goals is a foundational step in creating a roadmap for financial success. This comprehensive guide delves into the process of setting realistic financial goals, covering key considerations, strategies, and the importance of aligning objectives with your broader life aspirations.

1. **Self-Reflection and Values Assessment:**

   - **Identify Core Values:** Begin by reflecting on your core values. What aspects of life are most important to you? Consider how your financial goals can support and align with these values.

   - **Long-Term Aspirations:** Think beyond immediate financial needs and envision your long-term aspirations. This self-reflection provides the foundation for setting meaningful goals.

2. Prioritize and Categorize Goals:

- **Short-Term vs. Long-Term:** Categorize goals into short-term and long-term objectives. Short-term goals may include monthly savings targets, while long-term goals could encompass major milestones like homeownership or retirement.

- **Essential vs. Aspirational:** Prioritize goals based on their essential nature versus aspirational elements. Essential goals are critical for financial stability, while aspirational goals contribute to personal fulfilment.

3. SMART Goal Framework:

- **Specific:** Clearly define each goal. Instead of a vague target like "save money," specify "save $5,000 for an emergency fund within the next 12 months."

- **Measurable:** Quantify your goals to track progress. Use metrics such as specific amounts, percentages, or timelines.

- **Achievable:** Ensure that your goals are realistic and feasible. Assess whether you have the resources, skills, and time needed to achieve each goal.

- **Relevant:** Align goals with your broader financial and life objectives. Consider the relevance of each goal in contributing to your overall well-being.

- **Time-Bound:** Set deadlines for achieving each goal. Establishing timeframes creates a sense of urgency and helps with planning.

4. Consideration of Short-Term and Long-Term Needs:

- **Emergency Fund:** Prioritize the creation of an emergency fund for short-term financial security. Aim for three to six months' worth of living expenses.

- **Long-Term Investments:** Allocate resources toward long-term investments such as retirement accounts or real estate. These contribute to sustained financial health.

5. Budgeting and Expense Analysis:

- **Detailed Budget:** Develop a comprehensive budget to understand your income, expenses, and discretionary spending. A detailed budget provides insights into areas for potential savings.

- **Identify Non-Essentials:** Identify non-essential expenses that can be reduced or eliminated to redirect funds toward your financial goals.

6. Debt Reduction Strategies:

- **Prioritize High-Interest Debt:** If applicable, prioritize paying off high-interest debts. Focus on credit cards or loans with the highest interest rates to minimize interest payments over time.

- **Debt Snowball vs. Debt Avalanche:** Choose a debt reduction strategy that suits your preferences—whether it's the debt snowball method (starting with the smallest debt) or the debt avalanche method (tackling the highest-interest debt first).

7. Income Growth and Career Development:

- **Professional Development Goals:** Set goals for career advancement and professional development. This could involve acquiring new skills, pursuing higher education, or seeking promotions.

- **Side Income Ventures:** Explore opportunities for side income to supplement your primary source. This may involve freelancing, consulting, or starting a small business.

8. Risk Management and Insurance:

- **Insurance Coverage:** Ensure appropriate insurance coverage to protect against unforeseen events. This includes health insurance, life insurance, and property insurance.

- **Risk Assessment:** Evaluate potential financial risks and consider how your goals align with risk tolerance. Adjust goals or strategies accordingly to manage potential setbacks.

9. **Regular Progress Reviews:**

- **Quarterly and Annual Assessments:** Conduct regular assessments of your financial goals. Quarterly and annual reviews allow you to track progress, make adjustments, and celebrate achievements.

- **Adaptability:** Be adaptable in response to changing circumstances or unexpected events. Modify goals as needed while staying focused on the broader vision.

10. **Financial Education and Consultation:**

- **Continuous Learning:** Invest time in financial education to enhance your understanding of investment opportunities, savings strategies, and wealth-building principles.

- **Professional Advice:** Consider seeking advice from financial professionals such as financial planners or investment advisors. Professional insights can provide valuable guidance in aligning goals with realistic strategies.

11. **Integration of Lifestyle Goals:**

- **Holistic Approach:** Integrate financial goals with broader lifestyle objectives. Consider how financial success aligns with your overall well-being, family aspirations, and personal fulfilment.

- **Work-Life Balance:** Strive for a balance between financial ambition and personal enjoyment. Acknowledge that life satisfaction extends beyond monetary achievements.

12. **Mindfulness and Financial Well-Being:**

- **Mindful Spending:** Practice mindful spending by aligning purchases with your values and priorities. Consider whether each expense contributes to your overall happiness and well-being.

- **Gratitude Practices:** Cultivate gratitude for financial achievements, no matter how small. Gratitude practices foster a positive mindset and reinforce the progress made toward financial goals.

Setting realistic financial goals is a dynamic and iterative process that requires self-awareness, strategic planning, and ongoing adaptability. By applying the principles of SMART goal setting, considering short-term and long-term needs, and regularly reviewing progress, you can create a realistic financial roadmap that aligns with your aspirations and leads to long-term financial success.

- Balancing Passion and Profit

Navigating the delicate equilibrium between passion and profit is a nuanced journey for entrepreneurs seeking both personal fulfilment and financial success. This comprehensive guide delves into the intricacies of balancing passion and profit, providing insights, strategies, and considerations for achieving harmony in your entrepreneurial endeavors.

1. Identifying Your Passion:

- **Self-Reflection:** Begin by engaging in deep self-reflection to identify your true passions. What activities bring you joy, fulfilment, and a sense of purpose? Your passion is the foundation upon which a sustainable and gratifying venture can be built.

- **Aligning with Values:** Ensure that your passion aligns with your core values. A venture grounded in shared values provides a meaningful and authentic foundation.

2. Market Viability and Demand:

- **Market Research:** Conduct thorough market research to assess the viability of your passion-driven venture. Understand the demand for your products or services, identify target demographics, and analyze competition.

- **Identifying Niche Opportunities:** Explore niche opportunities within your passion. Uncovering unique angles or addressing specific needs within your chosen market enhances the potential for profitability.

3. Developing a Unique Value Proposition:

- **Combining Passion and Expertise:** Leverage your passion and expertise to create a unique value proposition. Communicate what sets your venture apart and how your passion enhances the quality of your offerings.

- **Addressing Customer Needs:** Ensure that your passion aligns with solving real customer problems. A profitable venture addresses market needs while staying true to your passion.

4. Strategic Planning for Profitability:

- **Setting Financial Goals:** Establish realistic financial goals for your venture. Define both short-term and long-term objectives that align with your passion and contribute to the financial sustainability of your business.

- **Diversification and Adaptation:** Develop a strategic plan that includes diversification strategies and adaptability to changing market conditions. Balance passion with a pragmatic approach to business management.

5. Monetization Strategies:

- **Assessing Revenue Streams:** Evaluate various revenue streams related to your passion. This may include product sales, services, subscriptions, or collaborations. Diversify income sources to enhance financial stability.

- **Pricing Strategies:** Implement thoughtful pricing strategies that reflect the value of your offerings. Consider the perceived value from the customer's perspective and competitive pricing in the market.

6. Building a Strong Brand:

- **Authentic Branding:** Infuse your brand with authenticity and sincerity. Communicate your passion through brand messaging, visual identity, and customer interactions. An authentic brand resonates with customers and builds trust.

- **Storytelling for Connection:** Utilize storytelling to connect your passion with the brand narrative. Share your journey, values, and the inspiration behind your venture to create emotional connections with customers.

7. Time Management and Work-Life Balance:

- **Prioritizing Responsibilities:** Balance the demands of your venture with personal well-being. Prioritize tasks based on importance and allocate time for both business and personal pursuits.

- **Setting Boundaries**: Establish clear boundaries between work and personal life. This ensures that your passion-driven venture does not overshadow other aspects of your well-being.

8. Continuous Learning and Adaptation:

- **Stay Informed:** Remain abreast of industry trends, customer preferences, and emerging opportunities. Continuous learning positions your venture for growth and adaptability.

- **Agile Approach:** Adopt an agile approach to business operations. Be willing to pivot strategies based on market feedback, evolving trends, and changes in your passions.

9. **Customer Engagement and Feedback:**

- **Open Communication:** Foster open communication with your customers. Actively seek feedback on your products or services to understand customer perceptions and expectations.

- **Iterative Improvement:** Use customer feedback as a foundation for iterative improvement. Make adjustments to your offerings to enhance customer satisfaction and loyalty.

10. **Networking and Collaboration:**

- **Collaborative Opportunities:** Explore collaborative opportunities within your passion community. Networking and partnerships can amplify your reach, introduce new revenue streams, and provide shared resources.

- **Supportive Ecosystems:** Surround yourself with a supportive ecosystem of fellow entrepreneurs, mentors, and industry professionals who understand the unique challenges of balancing passion and profit.

11. Legal and Regulatory Compliance:

- **Understanding Regulations:** Ensure that your passion-driven venture complies with legal and regulatory requirements. Understanding the legal landscape protects your business and contributes to long-term sustainability.

- **Ethical Practices:** Uphold ethical practices in all aspects of your business. Ethical conduct builds a positive reputation and fosters trust among customers and stakeholders.

12. Celebrating Milestones and Successes:

- **Acknowledging Achievements:** Regularly acknowledge and celebrate both personal and business achievements. Celebrating milestones, whether small or significant, reinforces your commitment to both passion and profit.

   - Gratitude Practices: Cultivate gratitude for the opportunity to pursue your passion while generating income. Gratitude practices contribute to a positive mindset and resilience in the face of challenges.

Balancing passion and profit is an ongoing process that requires intentional decision-making, adaptability, and a deep understanding of both personal and market dynamics. By integrating passion into strategic planning, maintaining a focus on profitability, and fostering a supportive environment, entrepreneurs can create ventures that not only align with their passions but also stand the test of financial viability and sustainability.

CHAPTER 5: NAVIGATING THE BUSINESS LANDSCAPE

Welcome to the enlightening journey of Chapter 5: "Navigating the Business Landscape." In the ever-evolving realm of entrepreneurship, mastering the intricacies of the business landscape is paramount for sustained success. This chapter serves as your compass, guiding you through the dynamic terrain of markets, competition, and strategic decision-making.

As we embark on this chapter, we delve into the multifaceted dimensions of navigating the business landscape. From understanding market dynamics to deciphering competitive landscapes, we explore the essential elements that shape the trajectory of a thriving venture. Whether you're a seasoned entrepreneur seeking to refine your strategies or a newcomer navigating the exciting world of business, the insights within this chapter are tailored to empower you with the knowledge needed to navigate challenges and seize opportunities.

Navigating the business landscape involves more than just reacting to market trends; it requires proactive decision-making, strategic foresight, and a keen awareness of both internal and external factors influencing your venture. Through case studies, practical advice, and actionable steps, this chapter aims to equip you with the tools to navigate the complexities of the business world effectively.

Are you ready to unravel the intricacies of market dynamics, strategic positioning, and adaptive decision-making? Join us as we embark on the exploration of "Navigating the Business Landscape," where you'll discover the keys to steering your entrepreneurial ship toward success in the ever-shifting currents of the business world.

Legal Considerations for Entrepreneurs

Embarking on the entrepreneurial journey is an exhilarating endeavor, but success requires more than just a great idea and passion—it demands a thorough understanding of legal considerations. This comprehensive guide delves into the crucial legal aspects that entrepreneurs must navigate to establish and sustain a business successfully.

1. Business Structure and Entity Formation:

   - Choosing a Legal Structure: Selecting the right business structure is a foundational decision. Options include sole proprietorship, partnership, limited liability company (LLC), corporation, and more. Each structure has distinct legal implications regarding liability, taxation, and management.

2. Registration and Compliance:

   - Business Registration: Ensure compliance with local, state, and federal regulations by registering your business. This often involves obtaining necessary licenses and permits.

- **Tax Identification Numbers:** Obtain the appropriate tax identification numbers, such as an Employer Identification Number (EIN) for tax reporting purposes.

3. **Contracts and Agreements:**

- **Drafting Comprehensive Contracts:** Contracts are the backbone of business relationships. Whether engaging with clients, vendors, or partners, well-drafted contracts clarify expectations, outline responsibilities, and protect both parties.

- **Non-Disclosure Agreements (NDAs):** Use NDAs when sharing confidential information to protect your intellectual property and sensitive business details.

4. **Intellectual Property Protection:**

- **Trademarks:** Protect your brand identity through trademark registration. This legal safeguard prevents others from using similar marks in ways that could confuse consumers.

- **Patents and Copyrights:** Depending on your business, consider patents for inventions and copyrights for original creative works to secure exclusive rights.

5. **Employment Law Compliance:**

- **Employee Contracts:** Clearly define terms of employment in contracts to mitigate potential disputes. Address key elements such as roles, responsibilities, compensation, and termination conditions.

- **Understanding Labor Laws:** Familiarize yourself with labor laws to ensure compliance with minimum wage, overtime, and workplace safety regulations.

6. **Privacy and Data Protection:**

- **Data Privacy Policies:** Implement robust data privacy policies, especially if your business collects and processes personal information. Address how data is collected, stored, and used to align with privacy regulations.

   - **Compliance with GDPR and Other Laws:** If operating internationally, adhere to data protection laws like the General Data Protection Regulation (GDPR) for European customers.

7. Securities and Fundraising Compliance:

   - **Securities Laws:** Comply with securities laws when seeking investments from the public. Understand regulations that govern fundraising, including the issuance of stocks, bonds, or other financial instruments.

   - **Crowdfunding Regulations:** If utilizing crowdfunding platforms, be aware of specific legal requirements associated with raising capital in this manner.

8. Environmental Regulations:

   - **Environmental Impact Assessment:** Certain industries may need to conduct environmental impact assessments. Compliance with environmental regulations is crucial to avoid legal consequences and contribute to sustainability.

9. Insurance Coverage:

- **Liability Insurance:** Protect your business from potential lawsuits with liability insurance. This coverage can safeguard against claims related to property damage, personal injury, or negligence.

- **Professional Indemnity Insurance:** Depending on your industry, consider professional indemnity insurance to cover legal costs arising from professional negligence or errors.

10. Exit Strategies and Succession Planning:

- **Buy-Sell Agreements:** Include buy-sell agreements in partnership or shareholder agreements to establish terms for selling or transferring ownership interests.

- **Exit Planning:** Develop a comprehensive exit plan, including succession arrangements, to facilitate a smooth transition in the event of selling the business or passing it on to others.

11. Regulatory Compliance and Industry-Specific Regulations:

- **Industry-Specific Regulations:** Be aware of and comply with industry-specific regulations. This includes health and safety standards, advertising guidelines, and any regulations specific to your product or service.

- **Ongoing Monitoring:** Regularly monitor regulatory changes that may impact your industry and adapt your business practices accordingly.

12. Dispute Resolution and Legal Counseling:

- **Alternative Dispute Resolution (ADR):** Consider ADR mechanisms such as mediation or arbitration to resolve disputes outside of the courtroom. ADR can be more cost-effective and efficient.

- **Accessing Legal Counsel:** Establish a relationship with a reliable attorney who specializes in business law. Seeking legal advice proactively can prevent issues and provide valuable insights into potential risks.

Navigating the complex web of legal considerations is an integral aspect of responsible entrepreneurship. By proactively addressing these legal aspects, entrepreneurs not only protect their ventures from potential pitfalls but also create a foundation for long-term success. Consulting with legal professionals and staying informed about evolving regulations ensures that your business remains legally sound and well-positioned for growth.

- Marketing and Branding Your Skills

In the contemporary professional landscape, the ability to effectively market and brand your skills is instrumental in standing out amidst competition and creating meaningful opportunities. This comprehensive guide explores the multifaceted aspects of marketing and branding your skills, providing actionable insights for individuals seeking to enhance their professional visibility and success.

1. Self-Discovery and Skill Identification:

- **Identify Core Competencies:** Begin by conducting a thorough self-assessment to identify your core competencies and skills. Understand what sets you apart and forms the foundation of your brand.

- **Passion Alignment:** Align your skills with your passions. This not only enhances your job satisfaction but also contributes to a more authentic and compelling personal brand.

2. Personal Branding Strategy:

- **Define Your Unique Value Proposition (UVP):** Clearly articulate what makes you unique and valuable. Your UVP should succinctly communicate the skills, qualities, and experiences that distinguish you from others.

- **Consistent Branding across Platforms:** Ensure consistency in your branding across various platforms, including your resume, LinkedIn profile, portfolio, and professional communications.

3. Building an Online Presence:

  - **LinkedIn Profile Optimization:** Craft a compelling LinkedIn profile that highlights your skills, experiences, and achievements. Utilize keywords relevant to your industry to enhance discoverability.

  - **Personal Website or Portfolio:** Create a personal website or online portfolio to showcase your work, projects, and accomplishments. This serves as a centralized hub for potential employers or clients to learn more about you.

4. Networking and Relationship Building:

  - **Attend Industry Events:** Actively participate in industry events, conferences, and networking sessions. Building genuine relationships with professionals in your field can open doors to opportunities.

- **Engage on Social Media:** Utilize social media platforms to engage with professionals in your industry. Share insights, participate in relevant conversations, and demonstrate your expertise.

5. Content Creation and Thought Leadership:

- **Blogging or Article Writing:** Share your knowledge and insights through blogging or writing articles. This establishes you as a thought leader in your field and contributes to your brand.

- **Podcasting or Video Content:** Explore creating podcasts or video content to convey your expertise in a dynamic and engaging format. Multimedia content enhances your reach and audience engagement.

6. Professional Certifications and Continuous Learning:

- **Obtain Relevant Certifications:** Pursue certifications that validate your skills and expertise. Displaying these certifications on your resume and LinkedIn profile enhances your credibility.

- **Commit to Continuous Learning:** Stay abreast of industry trends and advancements. Continuous learning not only expands your skill set but also positions you as someone dedicated to professional growth.

7. Testimonials and Recommendations:

- **Request Recommendations:** Seek recommendations from colleagues, supervisors, or clients. Authentic testimonials on your LinkedIn profile or personal website serve as social proof of your skills and reliability.

- **Case Studies:** If applicable, create case studies highlighting successful projects or collaborations. These tangible examples provide concrete evidence of your capabilities.

8. Crafting a Compelling Resume:

- **Tailor Your Resume:** Customize your resume for each job application, emphasizing the skills and experiences most relevant to the position. Use quantifiable achievements to demonstrate the impact of your work.

- **Include a Skills Section:** Dedicate a section of your resume to key skills. This allows recruiters to quickly identify your strengths and match them with job requirements.

9. Elevator Pitch and Personal Brand Story:

- **Craft an Elevator Pitch:** Develop a concise and compelling elevator pitch that introduces who you are, what you do, and why you're exceptional. This pitch can be used in networking events or job interviews.

- **Tell Your Brand Story:** Narrate your professional journey as a compelling brand story. Highlight pivotal moments, challenges overcome, and how these experiences have shaped your unique skill set.

10. Collaborations and Partnerships:

- **Collaborate with Others:** Collaborative projects with peers or professionals in complementary fields can expand your skill set and introduce you to new audiences.

- **Partnerships with Brands:** Explore partnerships with brands or organizations aligned with your expertise. These collaborations can amplify your reach and contribute to your overall brand positioning.

11. Attend Workshops and Conferences:

- **Professional Development Events:** Attend workshops, conferences, and training sessions relevant to your field. Not only do these events enhance your skills, but they also provide networking opportunities and exposure.

- **Speaker or Workshop Presenter:** Consider presenting at workshops or conferences to showcase your expertise. Being a speaker elevates your authority and visibility within your industry.

12. Monitor and Adapt Your Brand:

- **Feedback Analysis:** Pay attention to feedback from peers, mentors, and your audience. Use constructive feedback to refine your personal brand and communication strategies.

- **Adapt to Market Trends:** Stay informed about industry trends and changes in demand. Adapt your skills and personal brand to align with emerging opportunities within your field.

Successfully marketing and branding your skills is an ongoing process that requires strategic planning, continuous self-improvement, and adaptability to market dynamics. By consistently showcasing your unique value proposition, building a strong online presence, and actively engaging with your professional community, you can create a personal brand that resonates with employers, clients, and collaborators, ultimately opening doors to exciting opportunities in your chosen field.

- Scaling Your Money-Making Venture

Scaling a money-making venture is a pivotal phase in the entrepreneurial journey, representing the transition from initial success to sustainable growth. This comprehensive guide delves into the multifaceted aspects of scaling a venture, providing actionable insights and strategies to navigate the challenges and opportunities that come with expansion.

1. Strategic Planning and Vision:

- **Define Clear Objectives:** Clearly articulate your long-term objectives and vision for the business. Strategic planning provides a roadmap for scaling, guiding decision-making and resource allocation.

- **Market Research:** Conduct updated market research to identify growth opportunities, assess customer demands, and stay informed about industry trends.

2. Operational Efficiency and Systems:

- **Streamline Processes:** Identify and streamline key operational processes to enhance efficiency. Implementing systems and automation reduces manual workload, minimizing errors and promoting consistency.

- **Scalable Infrastructure:** Invest in scalable infrastructure, including technology and software solutions that can grow with the business. This prepares the venture for increased demands without significant disruptions.

3. Financial Management and Funding:

- **Financial Forecasting:** Develop detailed financial forecasts to anticipate resource needs during scaling. This includes projections for increased expenses, revenue growth, and potential funding requirements.

- **Explore Funding Options:** Assess various funding options such as venture capital, loans, or strategic partnerships. Choose funding sources aligned with your growth strategy and financial goals.

4. Team Building and Talent Acquisition:

- **Assess Current Team Structure:** Evaluate the current team structure and roles. Identify areas where additional skills or manpower are needed to support growth.

- **Recruitment Strategies:** Implement strategic recruitment strategies to attract top talent. Building a skilled and diverse team is essential for executing expansion plans effectively.

5. **Marketing and Branding Strategies:**

- **Reevaluate Marketing Tactics:** Reassess marketing strategies to align with a larger audience. Explore new channels and messaging that resonate with a broader customer base.

- **Brand Consistency**: Ensure brand consistency across all channels. A unified and recognizable brand enhances credibility and customer trust during the scaling process.

6. **Customer Retention and Expansion:**

- **Customer Relationship Management (CRM):** Implement a robust CRM system to manage customer interactions. Focus on customer retention strategies to retain and nurture existing clients while expanding the customer base.

- Upselling and Cross-Selling: Explore opportunities for upselling and cross-selling to existing customers. Increased offerings can enhance customer value and contribute to revenue growth.

7. Scalable Sales Strategies:

- Sales Funnel Optimization: Optimize the sales funnel to accommodate increased leads and conversions. Implement scalable sales processes that can handle higher transaction volumes.

- Sales Training: Provide ongoing sales training for the team. Equip sales representatives with the skills to navigate larger deals and more complex sales cycles.

8. Technology Integration and Innovation:

- Embrace Technology: Integrate advanced technologies that facilitate scaling. This may include adopting cloud-based solutions, artificial intelligence, and analytics tools to enhance operational capabilities.

- **Innovation Initiatives:** Foster a culture of innovation within the organization. Encourage employees to contribute ideas and explore innovative solutions that can differentiate the business in a competitive market.

9. **Risk Management and Contingency Planning:**

- **Risk Assessment:** Conduct a thorough risk assessment, identifying potential challenges and uncertainties associated with scaling. Develop strategies to mitigate risks and build resilience into the business model.

- **Contingency Plans:** Establish contingency plans to address unexpected setbacks. Preparedness for various scenarios enhances the venture's ability to adapt to changing circumstances.

10. **Regulatory Compliance:**

- **Stay Compliant:** Ensure ongoing regulatory compliance as the business expands. Stay informed about changes in regulations that may impact operations and proactively address compliance requirements.

- **Legal Consultation:** Engage legal professionals to guide on compliance matters. This includes employment laws, industry-specific regulations, and any legal considerations related to geographic expansion.

11. Monitor Key Performance Indicators (KPIs):

- **Define Relevant KPIs:** Identify key performance indicators that align with scaling objectives. Regularly monitor and analyze these metrics to gauge the success of scaling efforts.

- **Data-Driven Decision-Making:** Utilize data-driven insights to inform decision-making. Assess the impact of scaling initiatives on various aspects of the business and adjust strategies accordingly.

12. Customer Feedback and Adaptability:

- **Solicit Customer Feedback:** Actively seek feedback from customers throughout the scaling process. Customer insights provide valuable information for refining products, services, and overall customer experience.

- **Adaptability:** Maintain a culture of adaptability within the organization. The ability to respond quickly to customer feedback, market shifts, and internal challenges is critical for successful scaling.

Scaling a money-making venture is a dynamic and complex undertaking that requires careful planning, resource management, and adaptability. By addressing operational efficiency, building a capable team, implementing strategic marketing, and staying attuned to market dynamics, entrepreneurs can navigate the challenges of expansion while maximizing the potential for sustained success and profitability.

CONCLUSION

In the pages of "The Art of Money-Making: How to Turn Your Skills into Cash," we have embarked on a transformative journey, unravelling the intricacies of transforming skills into a flourishing source of wealth. As we conclude this exploration, it is my sincere hope that the insights, strategies, and practical guidance shared within these chapters have ignited the spark of entrepreneurial spirit within you.

We've traversed the landscapes of self-discovery, personal branding, and the cultivation of a positive money-making mindset. From uncovering your unique skills to navigating the complex business terrain, each chapter has been crafted to empower you on your quest for financial success. You've delved into the entrepreneurial mindset, embraced risk, harnessed the power of the digital age, and learned the art of balancing passion and profit.

As you close the final pages of this book, remember that the journey toward financial abundance is a dynamic and continuous process. The principles shared here serve as a foundation, a compass guiding you through the ever-evolving landscape of money-making ventures. The entrepreneurial path is not without its challenges, but with each challenge comes an opportunity for growth, innovation, and ultimately, success.

Whether you are a seasoned entrepreneur seeking to refine your strategies or someone taking the first steps into the world of money-making, I encourage you to carry forward the lessons learned. Cultivate a mindset of adaptability, embrace continuous learning, and let your unique skills shine as you navigate the exciting and rewarding realm of turning your passions into profits.

May this book catalyze your journey toward financial empowerment, allowing you to not only achieve your monetary goals but also find fulfilment and purpose in the pursuit of your passions? Remember, the art of money-making is not just about accumulating wealth; it's about creating a life that aligns with your values, aspirations, and unique skills that make you extraordinary.

As you step boldly into the future, may the artistry of turning your skills into cash be a source of inspiration, resilience, and enduring success. Thank you for joining me on this enlightening expedition, and may your entrepreneurial endeavors be as boundless as your imagination and as prosperous as your determination.